Printed in the United States of America
Published: by Legacy Voice Productions

Copyright © 2023 by Darlene Green

All rights reserved. This book or parts thereof may not be reproduced in any form, stored in a retrieval system, or transmitted in any form by any means-electronic, mechanical, photocopy, recording, or otherwise- without prior written permission of the author, except as provided by United States of America copyright law.

Cover & Illustrations by: Fatima Zeeshan

ISBN: 978-1-960179-07-4

To contact author for booking or ordering additional copies, go to:
degreen@cox.net

This book is dedicated to my lovely mother, the Honorable Alveta Valentine Green. Thank you, Mother, for being an outstanding Catholic role model throughout my life. Thank you also to all the Imani students that I have had the privilege of teaching over the years. May all of you always have faith in yourselves and achieve your dreams.

Hello, I am Curtis Kelly, a proud member of the Basilica of St. Mary of the Immaculate Conception Church in Norfolk, Virginia. My younger brother, Joe, and I are altar servers. It is now my pleasure to announce that this book, Imani and the 3 Rosaries, has earned our highest rating for books.

While reading this story, you'll be entertained and learn valuable lessons. The characters in the book include three best friends: Imani Brown, Carrington Mack, and my younger brother Joe Kelly. When Imani tries to replace the treasured rosary that her Grandma Rosa has lost, these best friends get an idea and work together to find a solution. Hint: delightful surprises occur at Grandma Rosa's birthday party.

I highly recommend this book for toddlers, children, teenagers, and adults of all ages, races, religious backgrounds, and nationalities. I am confident that everyone will enjoy this fascinating journey as much as I have, and that everyone will see the story vividly brought to life through bold and bright illustrations.

We at Kelly Book Consulting Services are thrilled to present this book to everyone: Imani and the 3 Rosaries!

Imani Brown lives with her Grandma Rosa and loves many things, most of all her Grandma. Grandma Rosa is named after the great Civil Rights activist Rosa Parks. Imani has the best grandma in the whole world who does so many nice things for her. Imani thinks that the greatest thing her Grandma Rosa does with her is to take her to church, particularly the 9:00 a.m. Mass every Sunday.

Imani loves her church, and she is proud to be a member of the Basilica of St. Mary of the Immaculate Conception Church in Norfolk, Virginia, because it is the only African-American basilica in the United States. A basilica is a Roman Catholic church to which the Pope grants certain ceremonial rights. Imani likes to see her reflection when she looks at the shiny white marble floors in her church. She is also proud and loves her appearance because she looks the same as her older cousin, Timiah Branch, looked when she was Imani's age.

In addition to looking like Timiah, Imani wants to be like her in another way as a cantor in the youth choir when she gets older. Imani, her Grandma Rosa, and the rest of the congregation enjoy singing with the large gospel choir in her church, as the choir sings songs that are deeply rooted in their rich African-American heritage.

Imani's two best friends go to her church. One of them is Carrington Mack. Carrington is a very good altar server. Imani is so proud of her friend, Carrington, and really likes to see her holding the candle lighter as she walks down the center aisle.

Joe Kelly is Imani's other best friend. He is an awesome altar server, too. Imani likes it when he is an altar server carrying the big cross while walking down the center aisle in her beautiful church!

Imani, Carrington, and Joe attend the same Sunday school class. Their teacher is Ms. Green, who is teaching the class how to use the rosary beads to pray the Holy Rosary. Imani is happy to learn that praying the Holy Rosary is an amazing way to become closer to God. The special sets of beads that Imani, her friends, and her Grandma Rosa use to pray the Holy Rosary prayer (with an uppercase "R") are called rosaries (with a lowercase "r").

Each student in Imani's Sunday School class has a rosary to use in class. Ms. Green has a large collection of different colored rosaries so that each child can select their favorite color. Imani selected a yellow rosary, Joe chose a green rosary, and Carrington selected a purple rosary.

Imani is excited to begin learning the Holy Rosary prayer because it is one of the most beautiful prayers anyone can recite. Imani knows that when she learns to pray the Holy Rosary, she will learn to think about the important events in the life of Jesus and his mother, Mary. Praying the Rosary brings Imani closer to the Trinity, which consists of the Father (God), the Son (Jesus), and the Holy Spirit.

Grandma Rosa has a golden sparkly rosary that she uses while reciting the Rosary prayer in church every Sunday before the mass begins. Imani thinks that the beads are the most beautiful ones that she has ever seen, and she likes to join her Grandma Rosa while praying the parts of the prayer that she already knows.

One Sunday morning while Grandma Rosa is reciting the Rosary prayer in church, Imani notices that she does not have the golden sparkly rosary that she usually prays with. Instead, Grandma Rosa is using one of the church rosaries that was in a holder in the pew along with the Missal and Hymn books.

After church when they got home, Imani asked Grandma Rosa about the rosary. She asked, "Grandma, did you leave your precious rosary at home today? You didn't have the golden sparkly rosary that you always use."

Grandma Rosa said, "Child, don't you worry about that rosary. Even though I've had it all my life, I can still pray to God without it."

The next Sunday, after their Sunday School class, Imani tells Carrington and Joe that she thinks that her Grandma Rosa has lost her golden sparkly rosary. The three best friends think, get an idea, and decide to ask their Sunday school teacher, Ms. Green, if they all can help her.

They ask Ms. Green if they could get a job to earn enough money to buy another rosary for Grandma Rosa. Ms. Green said yes and agreed to let the three best friends come in early and put the rosaries on the students' station counters before the Sunday School class begins.

After a few weeks, Imani, Carrington, and Joe have earned enough money to buy a new rosary for Grandma Rosa. Imani is happy because she can give it to Grandma Rosa as her birthday present. Ms. Green dismisses the Sunday School class early and takes the three best friends to the church gift shop to buy a rosary. They are happily greeted by the nice lady, Ms. Lamb, who manages the gift shop.

Imani explains to Ms. Lamb why she wants to buy the rosary. "My Grandma Rosa lost her treasured rosary, and I want to surprise her with a new one for her birthday. My best friends, Carrington and Joe, helped me earn enough money to buy it." Ms. Lamb is very kind and wraps the rosary in a very pretty box. Ms. Lamb tells Imani that there is a surprise inside.

On the night before Grandma Rosa's birthday party, Imani nestled all snug in her bed, while visions of Grandma Rosa's gift danced in her head.

The following Sunday after church, family and friends had a birthday party for Grandma Rosa in the church hall, and Imani was excited because she knew that she had a very special gift for her.
There were many people at the party, including Carrington and Joe, Ms. Green, and Ms. Lamb. There was a big birthday cake and lots of presents.

When Grandma Rosa got Imani's present, she said that she wanted to give her a gift first. Imani was surprised and said, "But it's not my birthday, Grandma. Thank you and I love you."
Imani opened the box and saw her Grandma's golden sparkling rosary.

Imani said, "Grandma, I thought that you had lost your rosary." Grandma explained that she didn't lose the rosary and had decided to give the rosary to Imani during the birthday party. Since one of the beads was missing, Grandma Rosa had taken the rosary to the repair shop to have it fixed. She told Imani that she had prayed with that rosary the night that Imani was born, which was also the same night that Imani's mom became an angel in Heaven. Imani had been very sick, too. Grandma Rosa said, "I prayed the Holy Rosary prayer with this rosary all night and had faith. When the doctors told me that you would be okay, I knew then that I wanted to name you Imani, because Imani means faith."

Imani gave her Grandma Rosa a big hug.

Imani told her Grandma, "I will treasure this rosary for the rest of my life! I hope you like my present." Grandma Rosa said, "I'll love it, child, because it came from your heart." She opened the box and was delighted to see two magnificent golden rosaries inside. "How beautiful!" she exclaimed! "I had a strong feeling that I should wait before replacing the rosary that I was going to give to you. It was God speaking to me. He knew that you were going to give me this dearest of presents!"

Imani said, "But Ms. Lamb, I only paid you for one rosary."
Ms. Lamb explained, "The second rosary was the surprise. I was so impressed that you, Carrington, and Joe got a job to earn money to buy one rosary that I wanted you to have an extra rosary to put in a special place." Imani said, "Thank you, Ms. Lamb, you are so kind." Ms. Lamb said, "It was my pleasure, Imani."

Carrington and Joe said while laughing, "Imani and the 3 Rosaries." Then Carrington said, "First, your Grandma Rosa gave you the precious rosary that you thought she had lost." Then Joe said, "Second, you bought a rosary to give as a gift to replace the one that you thought that your Grandma had lost." Then Carrington said, "Third, Ms. Lamb put an extra one in the gift box, so there were two inside." Together, Carrington and Joe said, "As you know, 1 + 2 = 3."

Imani laughed and said, "You two are so smart, it's three, just like the Trinity in the Bible, which is also three—Father, Son, and Holy Spirit. You two are the best friends in the whole world and I love you! You were so kind to help me earn the money to buy Grandma's rosary. We can each take turns using the rosary that Grandma gave me. I'll share it with both of you."

Ms. Green said that it might not be necessary for Imani to share her rosary with her friends. She gave Carrington and Joe presents. Inside the boxes were shining glowing rosaries in their favorite colors. Imani was so happy for her best friends. They all said, "Thank you, Ms. Green!" Ms. Green said that they were welcome and explained that she thought that it was very kind and grown-up of them to help Imani earn the money to buy her Grandma Rosa another rosary. That is why she wanted to surprise each of them with a rosary of their own.

Grandma Rosa said this was the best birthday that she had ever had—"so much love and kindness." Imani asked her Grandma Rosa if they could place the extra matching rosary on the grave of her Mother, who is an angel in Heaven. Grandma Rosa thought that was a wonderful idea. The next day after school, Imani and Grandma Rosa went to the grave of Imani's Mother and placed the rosary there and then recited the Holy Rosary prayer together.

The next Sunday in church, Imani, Carrington, and Joe sat together with Grandma Rosa. Each of the three best friends took out their precious rosaries that they had received at Grandma Rosa's birthday party and proudly prayed the parts of the Rosary that they knew with Grandma Rosa. Imani was happy to learn that her name means faith. Imani was blessed to learn how important the Holy Rosary prayer is. Praying the Holy Rosary prayer can make miracles happen, like on the night that Imani was born. Imani knows that whenever she prays the Holy Rosary, she is praying with others, because someone in some place in the world is always praying the Holy Rosary.

Imani's Cheer

Have faith right from the start
And always keep Imani in your heart.
Pray the Rosary and believe in your soul
That you can achieve your greatest goal.
So, keep the faith, as that's the right thing to do
And that's also what's best for you.
Believe in all that you dream
And remember you are on God's winning team.

Meet the Author

Darlene Green is an elementary school teacher in Virginia Beach, Virginia, and has enjoyed working with children for 25 years. She graduated from San Francisco State University and earned her teaching certification from Norfolk State University. She is also an award-winning storyteller and puppeteer and has been the president of D. Green Storytelling since 2011.

In the fall of 2018, Ms. Green received the President's Lifetime Achievement Award for her dedication to serving the community. She has volunteered for 4,000+ hours over 20 years to local libraries where she performs educational skits and hosts book readings for children.

Ms. Green, a lifelong Catholic, is a member of the Basilica of St. Mary of the Immaculate Conception Church in Norfolk, Virginia, and was inspired to feature youth from her church in this book.

Her church ministries have included Lector and Eucharistic Minister. Her most recent ministry is serving as a Rosary Leader. She looks forward to writing more books.